SANTA ANA
PUBLIC LIBRARY

SANTA ANA PUBLIC LIBRARY

PICTURE LIBRARY

TANKS

SANTA ANA PUBLIC LIBRARY

J
358.18
NOR

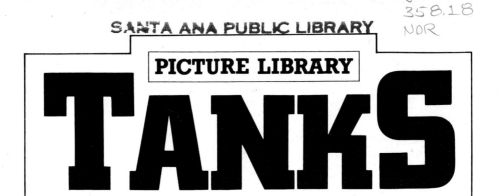

PICTURE LIBRARY

TANKS

C.J. Norman

Franklin Watts

London   New York   Sydney   Toronto

© 1986 Franklin Watts Ltd

First published in Great Britain
   1986 by
Franklin Watts Ltd
12a Golden Square
London W1R 4BA

First published in the USA by
Franklin Watts Inc
387 Park Avenue South
New York
N.Y. 10016

First published in Australia by
Franklin Watts
14 Mars Road
Lane Cove
2066, NSW

UK ISBN: 0 86313 349 5
US ISBN: 0–531–10092–8
Library of Congress Catalog Card
Number: 85–51456

Printed in Italy

Designed by
Barrett & Willard

Photographs by
Christopher F. Foss
T.J. Gander

General Dynamics Land Systems
Hughes Aircraft Co
NATO
Novosti Press Agency
Royal Ordnance
Swedish Air & Military Attaché
UK Land Forces HQ
US Department of Defense
Weston Simfire

Illustrations by
Janos Marffy/Jillian Burgess Artists

Technical Consultant
T.J. Gander

Series Editor
N.S. Barrett

Contents

Introduction

Tanks are armored vehicles used in combat. They carry weapons such as guns and missile launchers. Most tanks move on caterpillar tracks.

Main battle tanks usually have a crew of three or four men. They can travel on rough ground, climb steep slopes and turn around completely in their own length. On level ground they reach speeds of up to 50 mph (80 km/h).

△ Two US battle tanks, an M60 (left) and an Abrams. Battle tanks are used for making fast attacks across country.

Battle tanks have heavy armor and carry big guns. They are used to attack other armored vehicles and enemy infantry, and to support their own infantry positions.

Lighter tanks are used as reconnaissance vehicles. They check out enemy positions. Other tanks or armored vehicles have special tasks, such as carrying troops or laying bridges.

△ Many armored vehicles, such as this armored personnel carrier, have tank tracks and bodies.

The tank

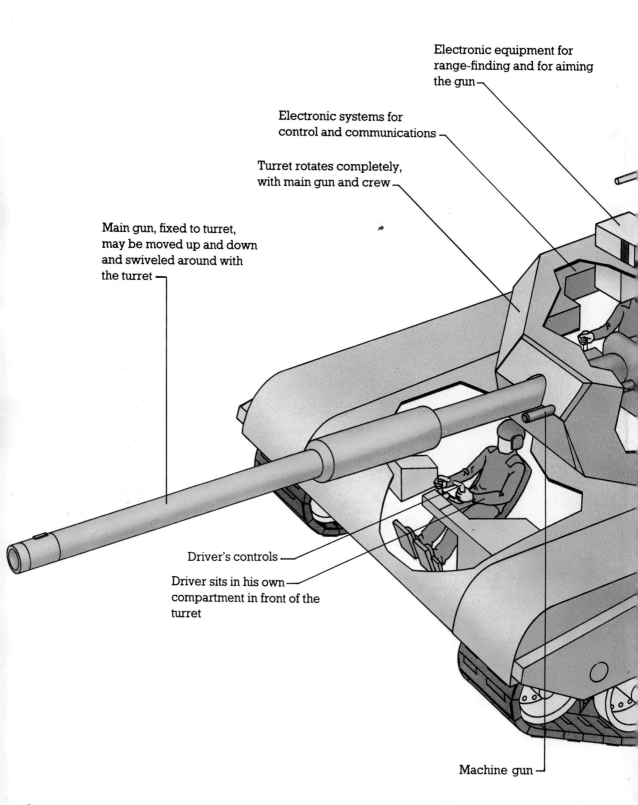

Electronic equipment for range-finding and for aiming the gun

Electronic systems for control and communications

Turret rotates completely, with main gun and crew

Main gun, fixed to turret, may be moved up and down and swiveled around with the turret

Driver's controls

Driver sits in his own compartment in front of the turret

Machine gun

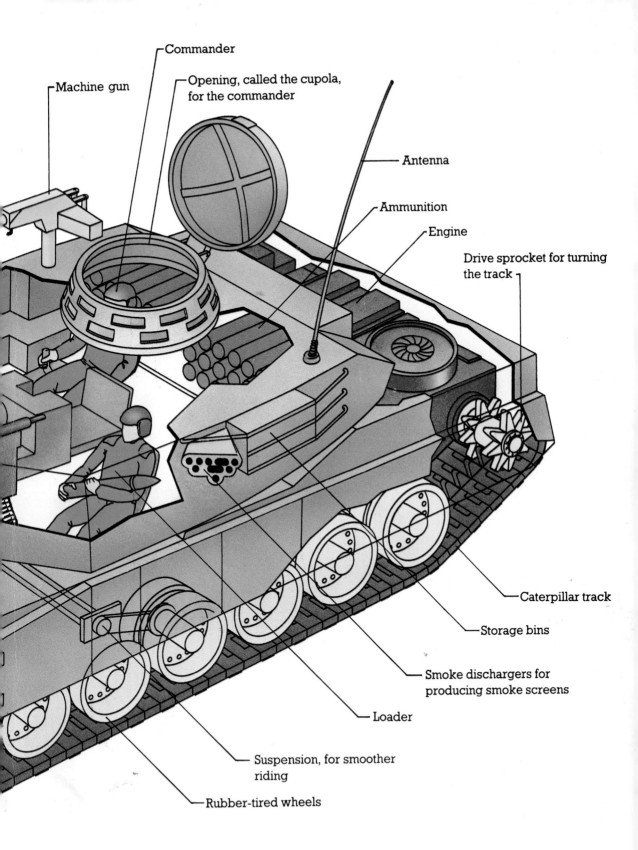

Machine gun

Commander

Opening, called the cupola,
for the commander

Antenna

Ammunition

Engine

Drive sprocket for turning
the track

Caterpillar track

Storage bins

Smoke dischargers for
producing smoke screens

Loader

Suspension, for smoother
riding

Rubber-tired wheels

Inside a tank

Crew members climb into their
tank through hatches in the top.
Once inside, they stay in their own
compartments.

Operating a tank in battle takes
considerable skill. The driver uses
a periscope to see ahead. Crew
members use computers and laser
systems to help them find and hit
their targets.

▽ An outside view of
an S-Tank. It is a
Swedish tank and has
no turret. The crew sits
behind the engine
which is in front.

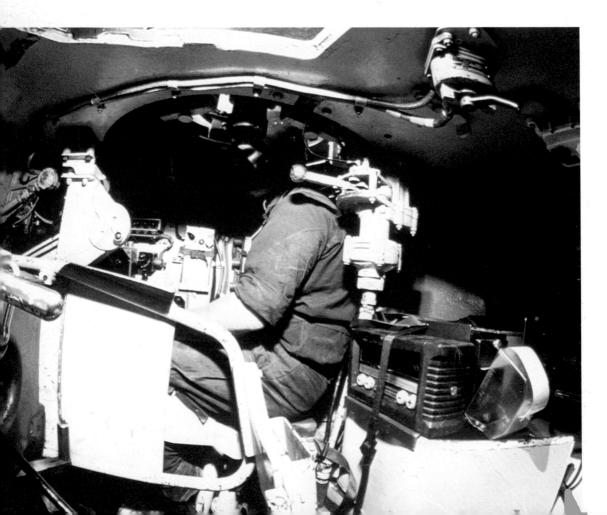

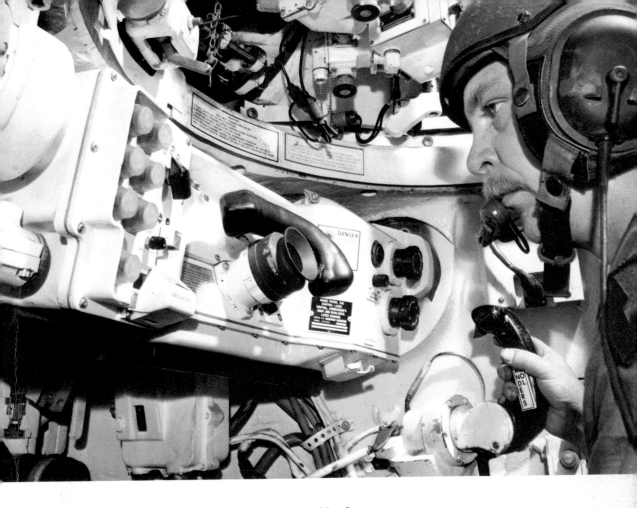

The commander directs all the tank's operations. He receives orders and takes action on them. He acts as navigator, reading the maps and guiding the driver. He also gives the gunner target and firing instructions.

In addition to his gun-loading duties, the loader might be responsible for operating the radio and preparing light snacks.

△ A crew member in an M60 studies a laser sight unit. This automatically gives him the target range.

Battle tanks

Modern battle tanks strike at the enemy from a distance. Heavy armor gives tanks protection as they approach their target.

Their chief armament is the big gun mounted in the turret. It swivels around with the turret and can be moved up and down. Most battle tanks also have a machine gun.

△ A West German Leopard 1 battle tank about to cross a river. The Leopard may be fitted with a snorkel, which can be raised to allow the tank to ford to a depth of 7.5 ft (2.25 m).

Battle tanks are heavy vehicles, weighing from nearly 40 to 60 tons. The heaviest tanks weigh about the same as four large passenger buses.

Tanks turn by slowing down one track. This gives them great maneuvering ability. They can drive over rough ground, flattening obstacles in their path. They can also travel through shallow water.

▽ A British Chieftain, one of the heaviest and most powerful battle tanks in action today. It can carry 64 rounds of 4.72 in (120 mm) ammunition for its big gun. The clusters of short barrels on each side of the turret fire smoke grenades to set up a smoke screen when needed.

◁ An M60 comes off a landing craft during an army exercise in Europe. The first M60s entered service with the US army in 1960. Thousands have been built since then and many other countries have used them, especially in the Middle East.

The latest versions of the M60 have many improvements, including a laser system for controlling the firing of the gun. The M60 continued to be the chief US battle tank until the Abrams was developed in the early 1980s.

The M60 in the picture has camouflage netting on its turret. The pipe sticking up at the back is to take exhaust gas from the engine out into the air when the bottom part of the tank is under water.

The most unusual battle tanks are the Swedish S-tanks, which do not have a turret. The Israeli Merkava battle tanks can transport soldiers. Some are designed to carry patients on stretchers.

The latest Soviet battle tanks have automatic gun loading, so they need a crew of only three.

Most tanks run on diesel fuel. The Abrams, a US tank, has a gas turbine engine.

△ The latest Soviet tanks are paraded in Red Square, Moscow. These are T72s, some versions of which have been named T80s by Western military experts. The Soviets do not publish full details of their fighting vehicles.

△ The S-Tank was designed as a defensive vehicle. Its full name is the Stridsvagn 103. It was made without a turret so that it can lie low. The gun is mounted on the chassis, or body. It is aimed by moving the tank up or down, or from side to side.

▷ The French AMX30 is the lightest of the battle tanks used by NATO (North Atlantic Treaty Organization), the Western military alliance.

Anti-tank weapons

Guided missiles are extremely effective anti-tank weapons. These may be fired from the ground or the air. They may be guided by radar, laser or infrared beams. Heat-seeking missiles "recognize" their tank targets by the heat given off.

Powerful guns, such as those on battle tanks, can penetrate another tank's armor. Mines are also used to put tanks out of action.

▽ A tank under threat from a guided missile. This anti-tank weapon is a Copperhead. It is fired from a gun and is guided by signals which move its fins, directing it to the target.

Reconnaissance tanks

Modern light tanks are usually called reconnaissance tanks. Their chief task is to report on the enemy's strength and position.

Different kinds of reconnaissance tanks are used by the armies of the world. Many are also used for other purposes, such as carrying troops or supplies or for attacking lightly defended positions.

▽ The Scorpion is a light British tank. This one is patrolling a river in Belize, in Central America. The Scorpion has aluminum armor to reduce its weight and give it greater speed and maneuverability.

The main armament of reconnaissance tanks ranges from a light cannon to a gun nearly as big as that on some battle tanks. Some reconnaissance tanks carry anti-tank missiles.

The type of light tank an army uses depends on the kind of terrain, or land, over which it travels. Some tanks are amphibious – that is, they can travel in water as well as on land.

△ M551 Sheridans taking part in an exercise at Fort Stewart, Georgia.

Other armored vehicles

In addition to battle and reconnaissance tanks, there are various other kinds of armored vehicles. Many of those have tank tracks and bodies.

Armored vehicles include anti-aircraft tanks, which provide defense against helicopters and planes. Self-propelled guns enable heavy artillery to be moved speedily.

▽ The Sergeant York is an anti-aircraft tank. It has an M48 body, with two 1.57 in (40 mm) Bofors anti-aircraft guns. The two antennas on top are search and tracking radars.

▷ A self-propelled gun on a military exercise in a forest in northern Europe. This is a Bandkanon. It has a specially built tracked chassis and uses an S-Tank engine. The gun fires 6.1 in (155 mm) shells. The magazine at the back holds 14 rounds, which are fed automatically into the gun. Further ammunition has to be brought by a supply vehicle. For reloading, the ammunition is picked up by the derrick on the back of the turret. The Bandkanon is controlled by a crew of four.

When an army is on the move, it needs special types of armored vehicles.

Recovery vehicles collect damaged tanks and other vehicles. Armored personnel carriers transport troops and protect them from enemy gunfire. They may also be used as ambulances. Some armored vehicles are used for putting up simple bridges or for laying mines.

△ The M113 is a US armored personnel carrier, or APC. It has a crew of two, the commander and driver, and carries up to 10 infantrymen.

◁ A recovery vehicle towing a Chieftain tank (top). The vehicle itself has a Chieftain chassis. A bridging tank (bottom) is used as a bridge or crossing. The tank unfolds the bridge and lays it across a narrow river or ditch.

▷ The M2 Bradley is an infantry fighting vehicle, or IFV. The troop compartment, at the back, has room for six or seven infantrymen. The picture shows a demonstration of the gun ports, or openings. The soldiers can fire special rifles mounted in the gun ports, while fully protected by the tank's armor.

The main gun is at the front of the tank and is also being demonstrated (right of the picture).

The Bradley was specially built for carrying infantrymen speedily to the field of battle. It can travel in water, being driven along by its tracks, and may easily be transported by air.

The story of tanks

Trench warfare

In World War I (1914–18), fighting was carried on from deep trenches. The opposing front lines stretched for hundreds of miles across Europe. Thousands of lives were lost in battles to gain a few yards of ground, because it was difficult to attack the trenches. They were protected by barbed wire and machine gun units.

The British set about developing an armored vehicle that could travel over rough ground and across ditches and tear down the enemy defenses. Secret trials took place and the vehicles were referred to as water tanks to hide their true purpose. That is how tanks got their name.

△ One of the first tanks used in World War I.

The first tanks

The first tanks used in warfare were slow, lumbering machines, moving at little more than 4 mph (6 km/h). But some managed to cross the German lines and proved their value as fighting machines.

△ French light tanks in action.

The first light tanks

To take advantage of the openings made by their tanks in battle, the British and French developed lighter, faster tanks. The most successful of these was the Whippet, which could travel at twice the speed of the earlier tanks. The Whippet had a raised turret above its body. It had separate engines to drive

△ Panzerkampfwagens rolling through France in World War II.

each track and was steered by altering the speed of one or other of the engines.

△ A Sherman tank fitted as a bulldozer for clearing wreckage from the streets.

Tanks in World War II

Tanks were developed and improved by many countries between the wars. They became faster and more powerful, and provided greater protection and more comfort for their crews. Tanks played an

△ A Matilda 2 followed by a Valentine. The first version of the Matilda got its name because it looked like a cartoon duck called Matilda.

important part in the fighting during World War II (1939–45).

The Germans overran many countries in Europe with their Panzer, or tank, divisions. The most successful tanks of the war included the German Panzerkampfwagens, the Soviet T-34s, the US Shermans, Lees, and Grants and the British Matildas and Churchills.

Modern tanks

The staggering tank losses in the 1973 Arab–Israeli war led some experts to predict the end of the tank as a fighting vehicle. A tank can be knocked out by a soldier firing a guided missile from a launcher held on his shoulder. But tanks still have an important role to play in land warfare. They provide the fastest method of advancing over ground and their computer firing systems make them deadly weapons.

△ A Churchill tank in action.

Facts and records

Heaviest

The heaviest tank in action today is the British Challenger, which entered service in 1983. It weighs 68 tons fully loaded.

△ A Challenger, the heaviest tank.

Decoy tanks

During World War II, both sides used dummy tanks as decoys to draw enemy fire. These were made of wood or inflated rubber and canvas. From a distance, they looked just like real tanks.

△ A dummy M5 tank, made of canvas and inflated rubber and used by the US Army in World War II.

Special devices

Tanks have often been fitted with special devices. Some tanks carry huge bundles of wooden stakes called "fascines" which are dropped into ditches to support tanks as they cross.

In World War II, "flail" tanks were used for clearing mines. Chains hung from a revolving cylinder at the front of the tank and "flailed" the ground in front of it. They set off any mines in the tank's path without damaging the tank.

△ A flail tank coming ashore from a landing craft to clear the beach of mines.

Fastest

The fastest tank is the Scorpion, a British reconnaissance tank. It has a top speed of 50 mph (80.5 km/h). The Abrams, a US tank, is the fastest battle tank, with a maximum speed of 45 mph (72 km/h).

Glossary

Armored personnel carrier (APC)
A vehicle used for transporting infantry to the battlefield.

Bridging tank
An armored vehicle with bridge sections that unfold or slide into place. It is used for setting up temporary crossing places.

Caterpillar tracks
The continuous belts that pass around a tank's wheels. They are made of metal or metal and rubber links.

Infantry fighting vehicle (IFV)
A special form of armored personnel carrier from which infantry can fire their weapons. Some carry light guns or guided missiles on their turrets.

Laser
A special light beam used in a tank's range-finding system or to guide artillery rounds.

Main battle tank
A large tank, with a powerful gun, chiefly used for fighting.

Periscope
A tube or box with mirrors and lenses that enables a crew member to see outside his tank while protected by its armor.

Reconnaissance tank
A light tank used for reporting on the position and strength of the enemy.

Recovery vehicle
A tank especially equipped with cranes and winches for towing away damaged tanks. It is often called an ARV, for Armored Recovery Vehicle.

Self-propelled gun
A large gun mounted on a tank chassis. Self-propelled guns may be moved around speedily. They are used to bombard enemy positions from a distance.

Snorkel
A tube that can be projected upwards to draw in air for the engine and crew when the tank is moving through water.

Turret
Rotating part of the tank. It includes the main crew compartment, except for the driver. The main gun is fixed to the turret.

Index